FAT POETS SPEAK 2
LIVING AND LOVING FATLY

FRANNIE ZELLMAN, EDITOR

FAT POETS' SOCIETY
Kathy Barron, Anne S. Kaplan, Lesleigh Owen,
Eileen Rosensteel, Mary Ray Worley
& Frannie Zellman

NEW VOICES
Durette Hauser, Deb Lemire,
Dr. Deah Schwartz & M.M. Stein

PEARLSONG PRESS
NASHVILLE, TN

Pearlsong Press
P.O. Box 58065
Nashville, TN 37205
www.pearlsong.com | www.pearlsongpress.com

Trade paperback ISBN: 9781597190794
Ebook ISBN: 9781597190800

Book & cover design by Zelda Pudding

The Fat Poets' Society is donating royalties from *Fat Poets Speak 2* to Ragen Chastain (www.danceswithfat.com) in support of her fat activism work.

"Sticks and Stones" appeared originally in *Breadcrumb Scabs Poetry Magazine* (Issue 26, February 2011) and is reprinted with permission.

ALSO BY FRANNIE ZELLMAN

Fat Poets Speak: Voices of the Fat Poets' Society
FatLand: A Novel | *FatLand: The Early Days*

Library of Congress Cataloging-in-Publication Data

Fat Poets Speak 2 : Living and Loving Fatly / Frannie Zellman, Ed.
    pages cm
  ISBN 978-1-59719-079-4 (trade pbk. : alk. paper)—ISBN 978-1-59719-080-0 (ebook)
  1. American poetry—Women authors. 2. Overweight persons—Poetry. I. Zellman, Frannie, 1954–editor of compilation.
  PS589.F383 2014
  811'.60803561—dc23
                                                    2014004070

To ALL THE VOICES SPEAKING OUT
on behalf of fat rights and fat pride.

Thanks.

CONTENTS

Poems containing extremely lush and sensuous descriptions are starred with asterisks.

INTRODUCTION 9

PART I
EXPLORING AND MAPPING: FAT COUNTRY 13
Fat Country *(Eileen Rosensteel)* 14
Landmarks *(Eileen Rosensteel)* 15
Topography *(Lesleigh Owen)* 16
Song to Sky *(Eileen Rosensteel)* 18
Stone Memories *(Lesleigh Owen)* 19
One Size Fits All *(Eileen Rosensteel)* 20

PART II
SEEING: COLORS OF THE FAT RAINBOW 21
Blue *(Lesleigh Owen)* 22
Fat Rainbow: Or, the BBC Gets Canceled *(Lesleigh Owen)* 24
Inner Evening, Autumn: Fat Gold *(Frannie Zellman)* 27
Inner Morning, Winter: Fat Silver *(Frannie Zellman)* 29
Valley of Purple *(Lesleigh Owen)* 30
Blood Poem* *(Lesleigh Owen)* 32

PART III
NEGOTIATING: DAILY MINEFIELD 37
The Separation *(Eileen Rosensteel)* 38
Weight of Life *(Eileen Rosensteel)* 40

Daily Minefield *(Eileen Rosensteel)* 41
Shame *(Eileen Rosensteel)* 42
On the Border *(Frannie Zellman)* 43
Myth *(Eileen Rosensteel)* 45
Morbidity *(Eileen Rosensteel)* 46
Sticks and Stones *(Eileen Rosensteel)* 47

PART IV
SAFE SPACES 49

Safety Net *(Kathy Barron)* 50
Yearning *(Anne S. Kaplan)* 53
Safe Space *(Eileen Rosensteel)* 54

PART V
BEAUTY 68

Tina *(Deb Lemire)* 56
Ugly *(Lesleigh Owen)* 60
City of Angels *(Lesleigh Owen)* 62
Fat Island *(Eileen Rosensteel)* 65
Apron *(Eileen Rosensteel)* 66
The Midway *(Eileen Rosensteel)* 67
Beauty *(Kathy Barron)* 68
Avalon *(Lesleigh Owen)* 70
Desert Life *(Lesleigh Owen)* 73

PART VI
MOVING 75

In Body Gratitude *(Kathy Barron)* 76
Fat Rhythm *(Lesleigh Owen)* 78
Fat Air Magic *(Frannie Zellman)* 79

PART VII

FLYING 81

The Really Friendly Skies *(Mary Ray Worley)* 82
Not Moving *(Lesleigh Owen)* 83
Airport Threat *(Eileen Rosensteel)* 86
Flying *(Frannie Zellman)* 87

PART VIII

REVOLUTION 89

Three Predators *(M.M. Stein—New Voice)* 90
Loose Women* *(Eileen Rosensteel)* 91
Acceptance *(Eileen Rosensteel)* 93
Veterans *(Eileen Rosensteel)* 94
Rampage *(Lesleigh Owen)* 95

PART IX

TO THE NEXT GENERATION 97

To the Girl in the Pool *(Anne S. Kaplan)* 98
Projection *(Eileen Rosensteel)* 100
The Cure *(Dr. Deah Schwartz—New Voice)* 101

PART X

LOVE 105

Love Talk* *(Kathy Barron)* 106
Love Play* *(Kathy Barron)* 110
Love Poem *(Frannie Zellman)* 112
Size Matters *(Eileen Rosensteel)* 113
Love Talk II *(Kathy Barron)* 114
Love Buzz* *(Durette Hauser—New Voice)* 117
Love Talk III* *(Kathy Barron)* 118

PART XI
FORGIVING 119
Forgiveness* *(Frannie Zellman)* 120
Soft *(Lesleigh Owen)* 128
Hope for the Haters *(Anne S. Kaplan)* 131

PART XII
GODDESS 133
Ancient Dreams *(Mary Ray Worley)* 134
Flesh Everlasting *(Eileen Rosensteel)* 135
The Goddess (Self Portrait) *(Anne S. Kaplan)* 136
Making Waves *(Lesleigh Owen)* 136
Radiance *(Frannie Zellman)* 137

PART XIII
ACCEPTANCE 139
Alice *(Eileen Rosensteel)* 140
Peace *(Anne S. Kaplan)* 140
No Competition *(Kathy Barron)* 141
Massage *(Anne S. Kaplan)* 142
Rainbow *(Lesleigh Owen)* 142
Whale *(Anne S. Kaplan)* 143

BIOGRAPHIES 145

Introduction

Lies

My apologies!
I didn't mean to trample
your lies into dust.

Lesleigh Owen

So here we are, in the second volume of *Fat Poets Speak*. This one is subtitled "Living and Loving Fatly."

Living. In this volume we poets talk about what it is to go through our days as fat people, fat women, fat poets. Before, in the first volume, we were voices coming to you, as the subtitle of the first volume indicated—voices you hadn't heard before. Now we introduce you to the way the people who own the voices live.

What does "living fatly" mean?

Of course we wake up, we yawn, we groan, we make breakfast, we go out to work or stay home to do and create. Like most people. But there is, to say the least, an extra dimension to living fatly.

Fat Country is a different land. It has some uncharted features and topography. And we see differently, sometimes more richly, in it. It also has minefields which we must negotiate and cross every day. Do you know—can you imagine—what it is to have people scream their dislike for you daily? Welcome to our world.

Yet as we come face to face with haters, we also come face to face with our own self-hatred and vanquish it. We learn of and honor the eternal woman, the goddess within and without.

And we love. We love fatly. We love from the depths of our fat bodies, souls and hearts.

Finally, we learn over and over to accept ourselves and to appreciate ourselves. Sometimes it is a struggle. Sometimes we find it pretty easy. We go through the acceptance process and procession daily and monthly and yearly and sometimes hourly. We negotiate our way through fat country, work up to loving and acceptance.

And we try, as well, to pass what wisdom we have gained, and the joy of acceptance, on to the next generation.

Two new poets have joined us as Fat Poets authors: Mary Ray Worley and Eileen Rosensteel. Mary Ray Worley began the Fat Poets' group in 2006, but was not able to contribute to the first volume. It is with deep joy that we feature two of her poems in this one. Eileen Rosensteel took a Fat Poetry workshop at a National Association to Advance Fat Acceptance (NAAFA) convention after the one in 2006, and began posting her poems to the group. Her poems feature prominently in this volume of the poems of the Fat Poets.

Corinna Makris, one of our Fat Poets in *Fat Poets Speak,* was not able to contribute to this volume. We hope that she will be able to write more poetry in the near future.

In this volume we also feature one poem each by our New Voices, fat acceptance activists who graciously contributed their work. They are Dr. Deah Schwartz, Deb Lemire, Durette Hauser and Mary Stein. You can read more about them in the biography section at the back of the book.

Those of you familiar with the first volume of *Fat Poets Speak (Fat Poets Speak: Voices of The Fat Poets' Society)* may notice that this volume is organized somewhat differently. Sometimes poets have several poems in one section. They may not have any poems in another section. This seems natural to me, since not only have we all come a long way as fat poets, but we are all at different stages in our lives and journeys. We are all comfortable enough in our poetic skins to be able to zero in on our concerns, our pleasures, our questions as fat poets and as people who live our days in a world in which we share the same hopes and fears as people who are neither fat nor poets.

You will also note our different poetic styles and rhythms—the way we cover our subjects, our diction, our imagery. Asterisks accompany the poems which treat love and sex frankly and fully. This is not because we are ashamed of our wonderful bodies and what they experience, but rather out of respect for those who are not accustomed to reading poems which offer such a wealth of lush and luscious detail.

There is also greater variation in length among the poems presented, from the three-line haikus to multi-page poems.

Lastly, you will see that after the introduction to each section we list the poets who have poems in that section. We also list the name of each poet above her poem. In a way this means, I suppose, that we are "privileging" the poet above the poem. I feel strongly that each poet here deserves to be acknowledged for her contributions to this volume and to be recognized and known for her particular poetic abilities and interests. I want readers to gain a sense of each poet, what she accomplishes and how she accomplishes it.

It has been four years since the first volume appeared. Much has gone on in our lives, some of it positive, some decidedly negative. We have all evolved, as has our poetry.

We hope you will delight in our living and loving, and that in our work you will see images with which you easily identify, and images which are new and startling.

Come live and love fatly with us!

On behalf of the Fat Poets,

FRANNIE ZELLMAN

PART I

EXPLORING AND MAPPING: FAT COUNTRY

What is it like, to dwell in Fat Country? How is one greeted? What kind of landscape does one find? How does one navigate? In short—what is life like? How does Fat Country differ from other countries?

Eileen, Lesleigh

Eileen Rosensteel

FAT COUNTRY

An actor puts on a fat suit
to see what it's like on the other side of the scale.
Reporting back to their audience
of common landmarks of Fat Country.
Discrimination, Clothing Challenges, Not Fitting In.
Tourist traps as trite as fat jokes.
Never exiting the highways to explore
the back roads of the natives
where we have created space to breathe.
Lovers that adore all of us,
Strength to stand out,
Friendships that cushion us.
Places not on any tour.
But my fat does not unzip and
I know all the native places of my neighborhood.

Eileen Rosensteel

LANDMARKS

I'll take you on the ten-cent tour.
Pointing out the landmarks
along the way.
The various dimples are inviting;
that's a ticklish spot on the nape of the neck.
Hold on tight if you go there.
On the left hand is the fading scar from childhood
drama
and the stretch marks make crisscrossing patterns
over the vast expanse of white belly.
Take your time exploring the landscape.
We have all the time in the world.

Lesleigh Owen

TOPOGRAPHY

I travel the city,
a fat body writ large
with streets for veins
and hills
and grassy knolls
with clumps
of brackish fragrance.

Yellow grass crackles underfoot
while a sky, blue as weeping eyes,
presses down,
a glossy windowpane.
Pathways wind and lead and
devour,
like thighs, always leading inward,
beige gradually darkening:

a tunnel, a turnpike.
I can't see where to go
but don't always
feel lost.

The wind trembles against me,
sighs up my skirt,
a breath of life
that steals my words.

Leafless trees groan upward,
thorns piercing dimpled flesh.

Brown-gray, the ground
shudders beneath
spills of acorns.

The terrain is too rugged for flowers,
though red roses hang upside-down,
spent and drying.
Earth cracks and crumbles
while short, plump fingers
caress, untangle, untie
knotted clouds.

Three months ago, I moved away
from California but
no closer to Florida.
Middle ground, middle
and open my mouth wide
to breathe comfort
and actions into words
and in those moments,
I can almost taste the bottom
of the world.

Eileen Rosensteel

SONG TO SKY

Let me be the mountain to your sky.
I will ground you, hold you steady.
Blow where you need,
I will be here.
Massive, unmovable.
You who are the holder of
      sun and moon
      steady and shifting.
I am the earth
      fertile and rocky
      stretching up to meet you.
The sky may never know the depths of me.
The way down roots of rock.
As I will not fly the forever arch of atmosphere.
But where we meet,
in the juicy middle
there will be life.

Lesleigh Owen

STONE MEMORIES

Within rocks lie
memories of plants, heat,
and crushing pressure that
coaxed stone out of flexibility.

With just a pillow between us,
their cragginess becomes a mattress,
a garden of moss and ideas.
My softness can flow like water,
carving with loving concern
canyons into questions,
rubble that sprinkles and roars
like stardust.

And maybe, when evening
soaks up afternoon,
rocks will sigh warmly and wetly
and
remember the scent of green.

Eileen Rosensteel

ONE SIZE FITS ALL

No room for me
in that space you created.
Am I supposed to twist myself?
Hold it, suck it in.
Pretend to fit
in the space
where I am expected.
Leave parts of me out,
dent my sides on walls
where I am supposed to be
welcome.

PART II

SEEING: COLORS OF THE FAT RAINBOW

We are taught to see colors in a linear way—so much of one color here, so much of another color there. But colors can swirl, become part of each other. Fat colors take on unexpected brilliance and glow, gaining in richness, vibrancy and complexity. These are the colors of the fat rainbow.

Lesleigh, Frannie

Lesleigh Owen

BLUE

Beautiful, bountiful, bright blue
blossom,
following the sun with your
gentle head.

In the salty nighttime,
Jupiter smirks a
path through the sunroof
while Van Gogh comets
swirl
in chunks of blue.

I remember the night,
stuffed with cottony fog,
when the moon
exploded from behind
indigo mountains,
a UFO intent on domination
and anal probes. We
laughed and
wondered when we could kiss.

And then we did and awakened in
a train station with
hot, blue-gray steam,
padded seats,
and destinations
beautiful in their fairy tale
familiarity.

I wanted.
I wanted to give you
the least carnationy
flower in the world.
I wanted to polish others' eyes
into gleaming
mirrors that reflect the rolling roundness
of your wavy ocean belly.
I wanted to sip your azure thoughts
and
eat each fragrant breath.

The moon stains my arm—
blue, with hints of magenta.
The ocean is a sea
of bright blue tears
and I
learned to swim with fat mermaids.

Lesleigh Owen

FAT RAINBOW, OR
THE BBC GETS CANCELED

This fat body doesn't come in
handy, nonthreatening shades of pink.
When I undress, no crisp sigh
gasps hermetically sealed air.
This body bellows through space,
crashing and rumbling
and stomping rainbows between
its toes.

There are times when I sit,
legs spread, inviting the air
to lick between my knees.
The brown between my thighs,
lumpy-bumpy
scratchy beardedness:
My very own chastity belt.
Locked against all those predators,
airtight unless I
say otherwise.
But sometimes
my knees part with intention,
feet flat,
thighs darkening like an
entrance to some
noisy seashell…

Seriously, what do you need, an Evite?

This body smiles
in ways you may not understand:
sometimes shy and ingratiating,
more often with heat
and throbbing redness.
This body,
where every corner turned
brings us pockets of the
pungent present.
Didn't you say god is in the present?

My partner's body spreads before me,
a platter of pink-tinged beige,
juicy like a Georgia peach,
round and linked
and always moving,
like all those patterns we find
while window shopping.
Beside her
sometime,
I look paler,
more cyan to her yellow:
Two candles flickering whitely
in fluorescent lighting.

I wandered into the hinterland,
a ghostly-pale mirage,
the roundness of my silvery body
a curved, celestial mirror.

Fat, white, 37 years old,
a transplanted Californian:
I flicker between

SEEING: COLORS OF THE FAT RAINBOW   25

invisibility and hypervisibility.
Grabbing your eyes
and squeezing them tight in my fat fist,
all the while
hiding behind this giant orange smile.

Screw "flattering."

I am round, earthy, and
sometimes crispy to the teeth:
an Idaho potato.
Sky-black mud
gnaws its way to my scalp.
Vagina dentata?
Those aren't the teeth,
yellow-streaked and sequin-bright,
you need to worry about.

Frannie Zellman

INNER EVENING, AUTUMN: FAT GOLD

To The Memory of Celia Dropkin (1888-1956)

The sun wasn't supposed to rise today.
They predicted rain and wind,
all the accompaniments of an autumn storm.
You know the kind,
where the banshee blows over the roof
and water howls from wherever
you avoid the sky.
Instead the early morning flamed so red
it could have been a happy fat demon
with wand, smoker and spikes.
"Sailors take warn," the saying goes.
Perhaps they did so
as the red slid into pink
with a tinge of blue at the edges,
then settled into a sun-culled lemon yellow.

It chose to drizzle.
Then at evening
deep and serious red and gold
erupted in a celestial *coup d'etat*
as if to inform above
that color was the new religion.
If this is the case,
then you choose red purples and orange blues
for morality
and greenish shaded mauve
for ethics,

perhaps the glorious fat swan
over the barely visible
crescent moon
for group identity.

At last light
in a particular spot
on Gardiner Street
the trees and lamps
fall to the same
softly faded
corn dream.

So close to night
the hour comes
that it begs a new season's time.
Call it inner autumn,
the fattest glad gold
you've never imagined.

Frannie Zellman

INNER MORNING, WINTER: FAT SILVER

Here is the sidewalk
where the cats wait
for their lives to line up.
You can hear them before dawn,
crying in their sex play
and pushing garbage cans
to see if food spills out.
Their night eyes follow yours.

Here is the road.
Late night pulls free
as your thighs whip against
each other, soft heat against
the wind, full and round
as hope.

Here is the bridge.
The moment always hurts
when silent lead sky parts suddenly
and grey yields to a wash
of sun that splits ice.
Plagues your eyes
with a new color: fat silver,
that only erupts inside.

Lesleigh Owen

VALLEY OF PURPLE

I walked in the valley of purple,
its scents of irises, grape juice,
and Halloween.
Dawn spread through the sky
like a fat woman's luscious thighs,
parting for a lover's gaze.

Violets prostrated themselves
beneath me,
each blossom a note in the
song of my step
while grass blades
kissed my soles.

My breasts,
soft and round like grapes,
sung and swung
and tasted the sun.
The bees followed my movement
with adoring eyes.

I loved the hummingbirds.
I am too grand to flit—
my footsteps send the
Earth spinning round the sun.

And the moon.
She slept and dreamt
of lovers as round

as
the seasons,
February's twinkling amethysts,
karma,
and me.

Lesleigh Owen

BLOOD POEM*

I want to write a poem about blood,
filled to the edge of the paper with gore
that slops and drops viscous tears—
that detergent can just never get out—
onto shoes, carpet, feet, arms,
anywhere bright and visible,
because I guess my words,
as shiny and creamy
as adipose
or plasma,
just aren't grisly enough.

But this isn't some goth poem.
I wear bright colors and laugh a lot
and do my hair up with
soccer mom practicality,
though no seven-pound, hairless human
has ever dropped from my vagina
and onto cold tiles.

I'm pretty funny in my job;
my students giggle all the time, even when
I show them studies about starving families
and animal abuse and corporate welfare
while scrubbing words like
"bootstraps" and "reverse racism"
from their vocabularies.
I have five ear piercings
but only ever wear earrings in two.

Definitely not a goth poem.

This is still a poem about blood.
Maybe because I love red,
treasure the way it consumes and glows,
how it curls to the edges of the floor,
light gleaming in crescents along its opaque surface.
(I mean, really, people, why else would I love red?)
Or maybe because I've been bleeding lately,
patterns of words and silence leaking
from a hundred small wounds,
some shallow and lipless,
smiles on my skin like fading Cheshire Cat grins,
some as deep and empty as South Dakota, as political
rhetorics,
as warm, bloody vaginas that seem to hurt and confuse
as often as they birth and heal.

I hate to sound all teenaged angsty—
you know, writing a poem with words like
"death" and "darkness" and "pain."
All those poems with lower-case *is*.
I figured I left that all behind
when I was a teen,
back when my whole
life curved outward,
offering every bit of myself up for public
scrutiny, discussion, dissection.
You wanted a confidante,
a partner in crime,
a blowjob?
I was your girl.

And now, my body and my words
belong to me—
mostly.
And I would only offer a blowjob now
after lining my tongue with barbed wire.
See? I told you it was all about the blood.
I guess I sound like an angry lesbian
or maybe a "multidimensional, overeducated queer
suffering the pangs of patriarchy."
And yes.

Wait. I'm wandering a bit.
I'm not pissed at patriarchy.
Well, okay, I am, but that's a constant,
an itch that, as Jules would say,
you just can't scratch on your own.
I'm mad at other things.
Mostly, right now, how a 420-pound body
that contains ten pints of blood
can continue bleeding liquid without
color, without
substance and volume.
Maybe if I write on my body,
cover it with enough Sharpie tattoos,
some of it might show up,
bleed through, if you will,
and I can garner all the
attention and concern.
Because, you know, I'm not a baby
anymore,
and my cries are now called "whining."

You know what?

Even optimists get hurt and idealists
feel depression.
I'm not oblivious to others' cruelty,
can't turn every moldy lemon
into a fucking meringue pie.
Yes, I cradle humanity to
my bosom,
suckle them all with hope and validation,
behave all Dalai Lama,
be-the-change-you-wish-to-see.
But, like Shylock, although maybe not so Jewish
(Hell, I can't even write "I love you" in Hebrew
without it looking like
a mathematical equation),
if you prick me, do I not gush blood,
a silent, anxious, colorless geyser,
warm like bathwater and affirmations
all over your butcher's apron?

PART III

NEGOTIATING:
DAILY MINEFIELD

As fat people, fat poets, every day that we come into contact with others, we negotiate minefields. Sometimes the mines, the traps, are out in the open and it is possible to avoid them. But sometimes the mines are hidden, oblique, difficult to second guess or avoid. These are the times and places in which we must summon strength to cross, to thread our way at times, to find the self-control to not let ourselves be either belittled or conquered by the mines, the detritus of the war on fat people raging across the land. We hold ourselves taut, in readiness, surmount the dangers—and keep on walking. Sometimes we have kept enough of ourselves unscathed to hold our heads up, high and proud. Sometimes it is simply enough to walk on, knowing that we have survived another attempt to bring us down, knowing that we have lived to love another day, somehow. And sometimes the minefields are completely inside, and of our own making, as we try to reconcile our bodies and selves with what we are told is "normal," but then refuse to give into other people's expectations.

Eileen, Lesleigh, Frannie

Eileen Rosensteel

THE SEPARATION

My body and me?
We've separated.
I didn't mean to lose contact.
But it was a troubled relationship.
I still have my head and hands.
But the rest of it—
I'm not quite sure where she went.
Periodically, I will get an angry email from my back or feet
fed up with overwork.
Or a "Wish you were here" postcard
during visits from my lover.

Body is very needy.
And I had other things to do
rather than listen to her constant complaining.
Besides, you should hear how people talk about her.
She has a very bad reputation.
We tried to make it work for years.
Counseling, behavior modification,
medications, threats, tears.
None of it worked.
Body was not able to permanently change.

So I found other things to focus on.
My family, friends, career.
My life is very full.
I wish she could've changed,
gotten into an acceptable shape.

She just didn't seem to care what I wanted.
It can be awkward when someone asks me about her.
I smile and answer vaguely,
"Oh, fine. Doing just fine."
I hope someday Body finds a way to change.
But until that happens,
I'm sure the separation is for the best.

Eileen Rosensteel

WEIGHT OF LIFE

Can't wait to grow up.
Drive, graduate, move on.
Watch your weight.
Wait till marriage.
In lines, in traffic, on hold
weight of responsibilities and regrets
pile up on top of freshman fifteen and baby weight.
Wait on partners, children, customers
for promotions, paychecks, vacations.
Wait for the kids to move out, house paid off, retirement.
Wait for visitors, nurses, doctors
until the wait is over.

Eileen Rosensteel

Daily Minefield

To step out of the house is to enter the field of battle.
Risk drive-by humiliation,
men in cars shouting
"Hey piggy! You're sooo fat!"
Manage to get on the bus to face machine gun glares of
judgment
for taking up too much room in the seat.
Get to work and climb the stairs
like a tank rolling up a beach.
Arrive at your desk sweating and panting
to be perky and welcoming on the front line
while dodging the helpful suggestions of miracle weight
loss cures
from people waiting.
Open your email to see the latest propaganda piece
in the "War on Obesity."
Thinking about your last checkup when your doctor
recommended
today's chemical weapon of choice
despite the scars you bear from the fen-phen assault.
Escape at the end of the day to the gym
trying to quietly relax and reduce stress.
But find your gentle water aerobics class has
been invaded by a drill sergeant shouting
about how many calories you are burning and
"Take it up to double time!"
Finally arrive home,
decide not to turn the TV on.
There is no way you could face
the firing squad of commercials tonight.

Eileen Rosensteel

SHAME

The name of the game is blame,
pointing fingers play dodge ball with responsibility.
Shame prescribed in the name of health
with diet and exercise, the junk food of diet industry
science.
Let's aim our anger at the schools, teaching same is better
than truth
and safety lies in uniformity.
Blame the media's digitally enhanced images filled with
empty famous role models
teaching us to view our bodies with judgment.
Isn't it a shame?

Frannie Zellman

On the Border

Catch the eye
of the guard,
then throw it back
and walk your thick legs
as nonchalantly as you know how,
skimming the grass,
barely sanding the dirt road,
considering the guard houses
as casually
as if they were bungalows
in a summer colony.

Send his scrutiny back
as if there were no question
that scrutiny was needed,
as if your eyes, balancing
above the void,
gushed innocence
and privileged ignorance.

They might as well say it out loud:
You have no right here.

The border guard morphs into
the *maître d,* who takes things in hand
and says, his mouth curling,
"Can we help you?"

No excuse.

The border's been breached.
Helplessly he looks at the waitress.
"This way," she says,
the table is near the kitchen.
Noisy, but you're seated.

Don't worry.
They will recoup
and write their anger in code
on the check.

Eileen Rosensteel

Myth

The story is told at your mother's knee—
how wonderful your life will be when you are thin.
Your pretty face will shift into beauty.
Awkward and shy transformed into grace and wit,
belle of the ball is what you will be when you are thin.
The myth is passed along in your doctor's office—
knees and hips move painlessly,
diseases from arthritis to West Nile virus avoided—
when you are thin it's as if you will live forever.
TV and magazines tell us stories of those whose
lives have been made perfect through the magic of thin.
Dream jobs, relationships, no more money worries.
Talents exposed when you are thin.
Worshiping at the altars of Diet, Exercise and
Willpower
built our culture out of the Myth of Thinness.

Eileen Rosensteel

MORBIDITY

It's not the weight,
it's the hate that will kill you in the end.
Carrying the fat around
may strain your knees and feet,
but the shame eats away
at your heart and soul.
Cholesterol in your arteries
hardens the walls,
while discrimination
shreds self esteem and respect.
And prejudice stops a life
faster than obesity ever did.

Eileen Rosensteel

STICKS AND STONES

Mall food court packed with
hustling moms, teens hanging out,
power shoppers pausing for fuel.
When one group of kids open fire,
a hollow point "retard"
hits the mom three tables over as she looks
into her precious baby's almond-shaped eyes.
Multiple "gay" shots
pierce the chest of the cashier
whose brother was beat up
for being a faggot.
"Fatso" bullets
silence a giggling group of girls
suddenly unsure of themselves.
The gang of teens head for the doors
throwing "retarded" grenades
at each other but only striking
the young man wiping tables
with their shrapnel.

PART IV

SAFE SPACES

As fat poets, fat women, fat people, we all imagine places, spaces in which no one would question our right to live contented, happy lives in our own skins. These wishes often occur after the days we spend negotiating minefields. We wonder how it would feel to walk through a city, a street, a room without being called names, insulted, or having people smother us with well-meaning but useless and sometimes harmful concern. We wonder how it would be to wear whatever we wished, talk whenever we wished, smile whenever we wished.

Kathy, Eileen, Anne

Kathy Barron

SAFETY NET

Could I create
a safety net of words
to shield against
the bombardment of negative messages
assaulting our bodies?
Could words ever do that?

Could I convince you of your
beauty and power and strength
and worthiness and inherent
and inalienable value?

Could I get you to stop selling yourself short,
compromising yourself,
trying to shrink yourself,
trying to "fit in"—
sacrificing your precious time,
your power, your life, your uniqueness?

Could we create a safety zone around our bodies
that doesn't let the shame that society sells
beat in upon us?

Like this:
These are the bodies we live in.
These are OUR bodies!
We don't need to change them,
shrink them,
or properly accessorize them.

We are not here on this Earth to be decorations.
Not here for your entertainment.
We are here to LIVE, to experience,
to enjoy, to feel pleasure.

We are here to dance—
not to measure the size of our hips.
We are here to eat and to laugh—
not to "shrink" our bellies.
We are here to make love with abandon,
not to hide or erase all of our so-called flaws.

We've got news for you—
we have no flaws,
just under-appreciated uniqueness.
Every part of us is vibrant with life,
ready to sizzle and pop
with joy and bliss.

We will NOT be disenfranchised
from our bodies
by the mandate to be thin, thin, thinner…
We can BE in our own bodies!
WE can LIVE in our own bodies!
We can celebrate and take pleasure in our bodies
exactly as we are!

Could I possibly stand here
as a Talisman
finding the right words
to give you the magic
to believe in yourself,

SAFE SPACES   *51*

to be your own compass,
to own your body
and your life?
That is my prayer every day.

Anne S. Kaplan

YEARNING

What I crave
   more than chocolate,
   more than sunflowers,
   more than 'most anything else:
     safe spaces.

Places without need to
   fight for my right to be;
   explain, educate, cite studies;
   sacrifice friendship or voice,
     just to justify my fat existence.

My soul aches for circles
   where everyone knows that
   value, goodness, beauty
   cannot be measured:
     only heart size matters.

I yearn for a world founded on love,
   filled with compassion;
   where differences are celebrated,
   roundness and angles both adored:
   bodies of all shapes and sizes
     glories of the Divine.

Eileen Rosensteel

SAFE SPACE

How do you build a community
        with people who have known little acceptance?
Rejected by those that are supposed to nurture.
Sanctuary betrayed.
Even the space inside their own heads
unsafe.
When bullies have microphones,
you can't even whisper.
We bring our wild, wounded selves to circle
        hoping for safety.
Building community, trust, relationships
        involves a bit of pain,
some blood shed as our rough, tender parts rub.
Daring to let someone hold us as we cry
        tears for us all.

PART V

BEAUTY

So much of our lives we have been told that human beauty relates only to a certain kind of body, one that perhaps five percent of all people on Earth possess. Besides being incredibly narrow, rigid, static and exclusionist, such an idea/ideal robs humanity and the Earth of so many other wonderful kinds of beauty that are to be found in people, animals and things. Fluffy clouds—wonderful thick breasts—softness in bellies and warm fat faces—furball kittens and puppies—woolen coats for winter—hefty and complex equations—colorful diving fractals—the thick electric air of summer nights.

Deb, Lesleigh, Eileen, Kathy

Deb Lemire—New Voice

TINA

Excerpt from For Beauty's Sake, *written in honor of the 10ᵗʰ anniversary of the Multi-Service Eating Disorders Association (MEDA), 2005.*

A baby girl is born. A beautiful cherub. Her name is Tina.
Look how chubby she is.
A little butterball.
Dr says, "Might want to keep an eye on her weight as she
    grows up."
Oh, you just want to pinch that baby fat.

Tina doesn't know Mom is terrified.
Should she breastfeed….bottle feed?
She'll lose that baby fat.
She's crying again—is she really hungry, don't want to
    overfeed her.
I wish I hadn't craved ice cream and Oreos.
First birthday cake smeared on her face, how cute!
Is that her second piece?
She'll lose the baby fat…right?

Tina is a chubby child.
    No one says "You're beautiful."
Kids laugh and tease her.
    No one says "Stop that—we don't treat people that
        way."
Tina is sad. Tina cries.

Tina is an overweight teenager.
    No one says "You're beautiful."

Tina eats chicken without the skin and grapefruit.
Tina sneaks chocolate bars in the back of her closet.

Classmates make fun of Tina.
    Laughed at in the locker room.
Picked last in gym.
No date for prom.
Mooing floats down the hall corridor.

No one says "Stop that—we don't treat people that
    way."
Tina is angry. Tina cries.

Tina is a chubby college coed.
    No one says "You're beautiful."

Tina looks for love. Tina doesn't date.
    Drunken frat boys are interested for one night; they
        take it whenever they can get it.
            Tina takes whatever she gets.
Tina eats.
Tina throws up.
Tina cuts.
Tina discovers amphetamines.

No one says "Stop that—you don't treat yourself that
    way."
Tina's lonely. Tina cries.

Tina is a plump young woman.
    No one says "You're beautiful."

Tina doesn't eat.
Tina is thin.
Tina is not.
Tina eats.
Tina throws up.
Tina is thin.
Tina is not.

Everyone says "Keep it up, you're doing great! You can do
  it!"

You've such a pretty face, if only—
We'll love you even if you are fat, but—
Don't forget to order a salad—
Are you sure you want that—
This is low fat, you can have it—
    This will make you happy, make you healthy, make
      you beautiful, make you loved.

Tina hears.
    Tina hears
    "You're not acceptable."
    "You're not front office material."
    "You're not marriage material."
    "You're not soccer mom material."
    "You're not normal."

Tina's heard it all.
Tina's read the books.
Tina's bought the shakes.
Tina watches Dr. Phil.
Tina's done the math.
Tina hates herself.

FAT POETS SPEAK 2

Tina loses weight.
Tina wants to eat.
Tina wants to scream.

No one says "Stop *THAT.*"

Lesleigh Owen

UGLY

I wanna see your ugly:
wobbly, jiggly in my hand.
Lights beaming down,
tiny stars,
O Holy Night.
I like my Solstice present
just fine.

I wanna hear your secrets:
speaking loud, brassy sound.
Slap my face,
cheeky wench.
Your soft tummy melts
like butter
in my mouth.

I wanna write a poem.
Uncap my tongue and let it flow:
sticky, shiny words,
sparkly wit,
wet, soggy rhythms.
I ride your laughs
like the sea.

I wanna taste your cocoa:
Cheap, brown fairy dust.
No swank for me.
I was raised in a trailer
and ate Cheez Whiz.

I like the ugly,
the forgotten,
the overripe,
the juicy, fizzy extravagance
that tastes
like cantaloupe.

I wanna drink your ugly.
Gulp it in and make it mine.
Sloshing, spilling over,
burning the roof of my mouth.
Unbuttoned jeans.
Woo woo—
is that the fire department?
Cuz I got my siren
right here.

Lesleigh Owen

CITY OF ANGELS

This steaming, sleepy, dark-skinned beauty,
no angel,
plump as a *concha*,
stretching in an arch over bypasses and dikes,
cooing like a mourning dove
seducing women and men
with golden-hued fairy tales
that smell somehow of dust,
hazy, lazy words
that clog the throat
and swirl like poison in the lungs.

She wriggles around us, catlike,
the strong, fat, craggy
foothills of her thighs and buttocks
looming under brown eyes and northern clouds
in the dark blue night.

Brazen, base-born beauty,
bleached by spotlights
into mottled, beige shadows
that writhe like cockroaches:
millions of ambitious, high-kicking legs
that dance, prance, and scuttle
in the halogen glare.

She sings to us,
through parched and cracked lips—
collagen-plump and brake light red—

a quivering Spanish lullaby.
We snuggle into her sun-warmed bosom
and wish for understanding,
a Mercedes,
Tex-Mex *empanadas*,
a tract home in the suburbs,
recognition,
adoration,
and privacy,
all frozen and documented
in the searing flash of camera bulbs.

The heat of her breath:
sinus-searing scents of exhaust
and cumin,
dark brown clots of earthy skin;
angels with shopping carts and cardboard signs
that flutter in and out of our busy awareness;
gleaming yellow teeth
that line impersonal and heat-frozen streets;
plump cheeks filled
with enough nourishment to sustain
ten million dreamers.

I know her:
her susurrant sighs and rubber shrieks,
her crackling brown hair and gray-paved legs.

You know me.
I am the one
whose tears turn the riverbeds to mud,
who fills my mouth with *sopapillas*,
who burns my strong arms in the sun,

BEAUTY   *63*

who wipes the mud from the streets,
whose ancestors painted the sky,
who sings loudly and off-key
about a just world
while dancing and swinging
my stocky, brown,
capable body
in the light of her ink-black eyes.

Eileen Rosensteel

FAT ISLAND

Woman-shaped island
floats freely,
water caressing curves,
soft edges
moving with the tides;
flesh forms a gently rolling landscape.
Belly laughs frequently shake
my Fat Island.

Eileen Rosensteel

APRON

My apron,
an overhang draping
my body like a soft white swag.
A bonus belly
that no one talks about.
Clothing fails to contain
whiteness broken by angry red purple lines
traversing my expanse.
Pressing down on my thighs when I sit,
reducing blood flow.
While giving me a
toasty warm muff to
tuck my hands in on
freezing cold mornings.

Eileen Rosensteel

The Midway

Spending a hot sunny day on the midway
holding hands as we walk
laughing loop de loops around the crowd.
We split up;
the seatbelts don't fit around my midway so
you ride the tilt-a-whirl
while I sit on the shaded bench,
guarding the giant stuffed giraffe.
We share sticky cotton candy kisses,
wandering hot asphalt paths with food on sticks.
Until exhausted, we retreat
to naps and showers.
Then we go to the amusement park
with perfect accessibility.
You find my curves thrilling,
with plenty of adrenaline rushes on this ride.
My midway has room for both of us.
Fun house mirrors in your eyes
show me transformed.
You pretend to be a barker:
"Step right up and take a look at this amazing pair of
breasts."
We both collapse in giggles.

Kathy Barron

BEAUTY

Fleshy arms embrace
soft breasts and belly cushion
an ecstatic hold.

Grasping my wide hips
nails digging into soft flesh
he thrusts into me.

I would not deny
myself one bit of pleasure
for any reason.

Cool soft flesh like silk
flabby inner arms delight
sensual treasure.

True beauty is found
in unique expressions of
our variety.

The joy of eating
shall not be mitigated
by false threats of health.

Pleasures of bodies
dancing, eating, making love
joyful abandon.

Pain teaches you things
that pleasure cannot show you.
What is your lesson?

Lesleigh Owen

AVALON

I'm thinking of a place,
bigger than a breadbox,
round like an apple with
bruises meant for
fingers and
gracious tongues.
They say its juice
holds the cure for many
post-industrial ailments,
but sometimes I
forget to believe.

I trekked there once
on accident.
I stumbled, and it
opened before me,
turquoise and orange like
a sunrise.
I tucked my large, fragrant
body in its grassy
bosom, slumbering while
branches raked grooves in
happy flesh,
a Shakespearean heroine
wrapped
in Titania's dewy skirt.

Elephants lumbered
and the stars spilled their

milk into my
enraptured mouth.

I awakened some
time later, head
lolling on a rock, sand
coating my tongue.
My hair had grown
slick, oily.
River-carved canyons
dented my face.

I looked and
looked and
called and.

Some say it lies in
a forest, others
the sea.
So small, maybe,
so delicate and shy, the
growling of my belly
frightens it,
the pressure of my words and
want
rub the feathers
from its wing.
So vast I am
already lost
within.

I sit
here, motionless,

a rounded triangle, breathing
the fog, chewing
the air.
I remember the taste of
apples, the smell of
water.
My fingers grow blue in
the starlight while
the magnitude
of my body
awaits rediscovery.

Lesleigh Owen

DESERT LIFE

They say humans
are 60% water.
They don't know about the deserts:
sagebrush, dunes, Joshua trees
so mighty they soak up the sunsets
and glow
like desiccated candles.

I was born in the desert
on a Tuesday morning.
The temperature topped one-oh-six.
My sisters drank from hoses
and baked mud effigies.

I stumbled through cities
like some survivor of the apocalypse,
mouth dry, lips cracked, eyes too dehydrated
to irrigate this dusty face.
I stretched out my hand,
burned and wrinkled with bitten, red nails.
They found their toes, their expensive
polished shoes,
far more fascinating than the
living leather shambling toward them,
a blistered reminder of their own
Mojave memories.

I stare into oceans and mud puddles,
those mirrors painting

pictures of rigid, angry buildings
making love to the sky.
Where is my face?
My belly? My legs?
Do my arms only exist when
clasping others in place?
Horizontal lines that order
letters into words,
words into rows,
rows into sentences—
life, if you must know.

I am a desert garden.
You may not know this,
may not see the tiny blossoms that
burn along my flesh,
bloom in the places where rolls overlap
and kiss.
We have learned to thrive in the heat,
grow fat and wise
eating sunshine
and sipping wind.
My belly smolders and tarnishes,
hills and valleys for all kinds
of quiet lives.
I am too dull to reflect,
too strong to waste parched tears,
too self-sufficient to sacrifice myself
for the benefit of those
who won't even learn my name.

PART VI

MOVING

Fat people are often discouraged from moving, not only by those who ridicule them, but by their own beliefs that they cannot or are not supposed to move, to take pleasure in movement. Given a halfway friendly environment and their own discovery that their bodies not only can move, but look wonderful in their soft jiggling and play, fat people can glory in feeling their limbs and bellies and shoulders swing free as they feel the air gently moving with them.

Kathy, Lesleigh, Frannie

Kathy Barron

In Body Gratitude

The sun kisses
my rounded thighs
as they pump strongly
up and down,
moving me forward.

The breeze envelops
my lush body,
swirling over freckled skin,
playing along with the kissing sun
as I ride my bike down the street.

Plump arms in front of me,
hands loosely holding the grips
guiding my way
as my belly and breasts sway
and my abundant ass rocks side to side.

Music plays in my iPodded ears,
pulses through my dancing body
filling me with joy and energy.
I pedal in time to the beat,
grinning widely.

And I am filled with gratitude
for this life and this day and this moment,
for music and sunshine and bike rides
and mostly for this body—
this beautiful, healthy, miraculous body

which allows me to experience so much pleasure.
Thank you, Body!
I am grateful and I love you!

Lesleigh Owen

FAT RHYTHM

I rotate, move,
shake, gyrate—
left to right,
right to left.
My boulder belly
rumbles and tumbles,
chasing boob one,
bumping boob two—
a
rockslide of rhythm.

Boom, boom, pow:

My heartbeat,
a bright orange wristwatch,
the scratch of
fat over bones.

Rat-a-tat bounce!
Slip-slap of slick skin.

We fat folks walk
a
syncopated
rhythm of round.

Frannie Zellman

FAT AIR MAGIC

Best athlete. But fat.
Moves quick. How? Corners fat air
magic. Stand away.

PART VII

FLYING

Flying is fraught with good and bad ideas and intentions for fat people. Some of us worry about how to fit in seats that aren't meant for real people, but more for stick figures. Others worry about the embarrassment of asking for a seatbelt extender and the difficulty in fitting into the economy-class bathrooms. Related: The person who, upon seeing he will sit next to you, makes faces worthy of a tragic opera. Related: Always beeping at the security check because the machine doesn't understand your luscious layers of flesh.

And yet—

If you can get beyond all this—and sometimes you actually do—there is the ecstasy of weightlessness, of feeling yourself gliding above clouds and time and space, for once not bothered by our solidity or some useless number on a scale. There is the shimmying through clouds, the chiaroscuro of light and dark and light again.

Flying can be painful. Yet it can also become the magic sector and dimension in which you free yourself from the demands and jeers of gravity. And from those who would confine you to it.

Mary, Lesleigh, Eileen, Frannie

Mary Ray Worley

THE REALLY FRIENDLY SKIES

Wide doorways welcome
ample travelers, all
carry-ons and hips and
boarding passes.
Clenched jaws relax
into broad smiles
as overweight fears
dissipate through
the spacious aisles.
Comfy seats lovingly cradle
suddenly unembarrassed generosities.
Elbow room, knee room,
wiggle room, giggle room.
My God, what prayer
has been answered here
that tray tables fall flat and neat
in front of happy, abundant bellies?
Hearts that were heavy with shame
rise, floating gleefully through the clouds,
the lightness of joy
bearing them up and up
to a new wideness,
a fullness that comes
only after years and years
of secret hunger.
All passengers, please
keep your seat belts fastened
and your hopes securely stowed
in the overhead bins.

Lesleigh Owen

NOT MOVING

I'm not moving.

I'm utterly still,
trapped
between humanity and plastic,
clapped
between air that hisses and shrieks,
snapped
between jaws that bite the dark meat
from my thighs.

I'm not moving.

No water or soda, thanks.
I know I'm squishable
and squeezable and all,
but I have no desire
to lodge myself into the
hard-angled, beige Barbie bathroom,
waiting for hard-angled, beige-skinned Barbies
to pop me out
like a champagne cork
and spill me back
in a humiliated tide
to my little piece
of purgatory.

Has it really only been
sixteen minutes

since I last
checked my watch?

I'm not moving.

Canned air,
cricked neck,
feet that have long since
grown numb,
armrest that carves
a meaty slice
from this rump's roast.

I am a physics problem,
a mathematical conundrum:
How to make a fat woman
fold inward
on herself?

What engineering equations
can help us squeeze
a 355-pound goddess
into a tot-sized space?

If an airplane
leaves L.A. at 3:34 pm
and travels at 523 miles per hour
to D.C.,
how can we justify
depriving a human
of her right
to comfort?

Five-hundred miles per hour,
and
I'm
still
not
moving.

Eileen Rosensteel

AIRPORT THREAT

Two fatties walk
side by side
down the airport corridor.
Before them silent prayers—
"Not my flight. Not my flight."
"Please not next to me"—
are flung to unresponsive airline gods.
Behind the women
brows are wiped
with sighs of relief.
Until their gate is found
their flightmates
aim dirty looks and
puff themselves up
to protect precious armrest real estate.

Frannie Zellman

FLYING

In those days before the flight
I dreamed the plane crashed
because I weighed so much.

Yet when I finally boarded
I felt wings.

I forgot weight, height, breadth,
volume,
time, day, month, year.

In sleep, radiance, now become aroma,
suffused what was once my body
and stole over the hidden stars
like the milky breath
of flowers.

On waking, dark.

Suddenly on one side
the plane exploded into sun.

And I, the flyer,
straddled the edge
of night and day

as if I'd been born
to stalk heaven.

PART VIII

REVOLUTION

Since the late 1960s, more and more scientific sources have been confirming what we fat people knew all along—that some people are meant to be fat, some are meant to be slim, and some are meant to be somewhere in between. We fat people have a rich heritage of revolting against not only unjust conditions and pronounced bigotry, but also against those who keep trying to make us into their favored version of cookie-cutter thin.

And yet sometimes just surviving to survive another day as a fat person without wanting to hide under the bed can be a revolutionary act.

Every day, fat people commit revolution. By living, by loving when we are told it is impossible for us to love anyone and for anyone to love us. By dancing. By marching. By demanding clothes that fit well and appropriately. By voicing our disgust with airline staff who treat us as less than human.

By being determined to push forward to another day.

M.M., Eileen, Lesleigh

M. M. Stein—New Voice

THREE PREDATORS

Quietly stalking,
consuming all in their path:
Loathing, Shaming, Hate.

Wolves prey upon sheep
that follow where they are led.
Some go their own way.

Strength is in numbers.
We turn and bite back at wolves
and we are growing.

Eileen Rosensteel

LOOSE WOMEN*

Loose women on a rampage,
running wild through the streets,
unbound by the rules of society.

My soft bosom and arms enfold
the crying child as I offer comfort.
The corners of my eyes and mouth
crinkle as I smile.

Loose women burst from their corsets,
building bodies of muscle and fat
unfit for feminine roles.

The skin under my arm quivers
as I draw back the bowstring.
My belly jiggles and quakes
from my loud laughter.

Loose women are dangerous,
refusing to be rigid or bound.
Strict regimens rejected.

My lungs draw deep breaths
to scream against injustice.
My womb expands for gestation
of children, art, change.

Loose women filled with passion,
drinking deeply from life.

Not caring about propriety.

The lush body of my lover
pulls me closer.
Curves, rolls and folds explored
until orgasm shakes the world.

Loose women on a rampage,
running wild through the streets.
Daring you to join them.

Eileen Rosensteel

Acceptance

Fuck your size acceptance.
I want a body appreciation movement.
I don't need your grudgingly given mediocre acceptance.
I don't have time for someone
who tolerates my existence like a charity case.
My body's a miracle, not a consolation prize.
I will not beg and fight for mere acceptance.
You seem to think that your idea of what a body
should look like is relevant.
It's not.
My abundance, her slenderness, and his girth,
their shape, skin color and physical ability,
are all independent of their worth.
Our fat asses can't be denied.
I will be over here in lust with myself.
Mere acceptance is too small for my being.
A force of nature doesn't wait for acceptance.
It grows, creates, loves and lives with abandon.

Eileen Rosensteel

VETERANS

Some day we will march.
We, the veterans of the War on Obesity.
Multitudes mutilated by scalpels,
damaged by pharmaceuticals.
We will stand up,
demand a cease fire.

One day we will march.
We, the survivors of the War on Obesity
with our eating disorders, disfigured bodies,
damaged hearts, minds and spirits.
We will heal.
Teach them a better way.

Some day we will march,
the survivors of the War on Obesity,
with the children taken from our "too-fat" arms.
Humiliated by those who should be protecting us.
Taught to hate ourselves.
We will take our place,
claiming our humanity.

One day we will march,
the veterans of the War on Obesity,
rejecting the hatred, fear and prejudice.
In a world that doesn't fit us and
doesn't want us
we will cry, "Enough!"
Demand respect.

One day we will march.
Today we will survive.

Lesleigh Owen

Rampage

What was that you said?
"Fatness is on a rampage"?
I'm glad you noticed.

.

Part IX

To The Next Generation

We want so much for you to live in a more tolerant, fat-celebratory world than the one in which we were raised. Our poems are our prayers for you.

Anne, Eileen, Deah

Anne S. Kaplan

To the Girl in the Pool

You walk by me in the pool,
    an image of sadness.
    As much as you seem to be
    trying to be invisible...
    I see you.

Your head down, shoulders hunched,
    eyes hidden beneath bangs,
    round body sheathed in solid black...
    I ache for you.

You return to your family on deck
    laughing, colorful, carefree, happy,
    and not a roundness among them.
    They're not like you.

Your story will never be known to me,
    but I do know being surrounded by family
    yet feeling so different, so unincluded.
    I know your alone-ness.
    I weep for you.

You and I never spoke a word.
    I didn't know how to approach,
    yet rue the comfort and hope I didn't share.
    Would you have listened to the fat old lady
    who cared for you?

You will come to know some things I've learned:
    That being different is more than OK,
    love and beauty come in all sizes, and
    your lifejoy asks no changes save
    your own beliefs about your loveliness.
    Across space and time,
    I celebrate you.

Eileen Rosensteel

PROJECTION

Stop showing your home movies—
"Mom made me eat my vegetables so I wouldn't be Fat."
"Grandma only showed love through food
and made me Fat!"
"Sibling horror stories—Lard Butt Bullying"—
on my fat white ass.

Stop projecting your videos—
"Big Mama takes care of the Little Bad Boy."
"Naughty Little Fat Girl gets Taught a Lesson."
"Fat Piggy Squeals"—
on my corpulent breasts.

Stop broadcasting your films—
"I was Fat until I found the One Thin Way!"
"Morbid Obesity. The Fat that Kills."
"The Thing that Ate NYC!"—
on my rotund belly.

It may look like a blank screen.
Perfect for your own personal drama to play upon.
But this is my body.
And your stories don't get air time here.

If you listen, I will tell you the stories written on this
flesh.

THE CURE

As a girl I was protected from the Measles
    and the Mumps
but not from the dis-ease caused by chubby thighs
    and lumps.
I felt dejected when rejected and not labeled as a beauty.
"Conforming," I was told, "is your moral civic duty."
My mind, however, knowing that I deserved respect,
instinctively fought back with its pre-teen intellect.

"People are different in so many ways—
 why are we judged by how much we weigh?"

But teases and taunts caused the virus to spread, infecting
    my self-esteem.
And in desperate attempts I starved myself in pursuit of
    the American Dream.
Self-hate is pernicious, infectious, distressing;
breathed in through the media and lack of caressing.
Once inside it multiplied, metastasized and grew.
And everything my mind once questioned my body now
    knew was true.

Things got worse as the monster within became the
    monster without;
Self-hate is contagious,
and what's really outrageous,
it's spread with the sputum of doubt.

As I grew and matured my self-hate endured

and I pushed many lovers away.
Though they may have found
me luscious and round,
I just didn't feel the same way.

His eyes looked at me with hunger and lust—there must
    be some mistake.
I've been told for so long
that my body's all wrong,
and my heart began to ache.
Then I felt in his touch the heat of desire
and without protection ran into the fire.
I was asked to dance, to revel, jump in;
but the virus reminded me,
"STOP—YOU'RE NOT THIN."

No condom to keep my thoughts tucked inside,
I passed the bug on when I started to cry:

"I'm fat and I'm ugly." The virus was strong.
"Why would you want me? You have to be wrong."
I tried to convince him, but he seemed quite immune;
at first he looked hurt, but then changed his tune.

"You've got it quite bad—we'll have to fix that.
What's wrong is hating yourself 'cause you're fat.
And maybe I'm wrong, but the logic seems hazy—
telling *me* how to feel about *you* seems crazy.
It isn't your fault there is no injection;
against media pressure there's little protection.
But your case isn't terminal, of that I am clear;
self-esteem class is starting right now and right here.

Beauty is not just one shape or one size,
and no one can tell me what makes *my* "you know what"
  rise.

I laughed and added, "It's so complicated.
The importance of beauty is way overrated.
Carving and starving ourselves to fit in,
and still we are either too fat or too thin."

So we talked and we drank and we romped until dawn,
and the rest I'll leave out 'cause it borders on porn.
And while it didn't happen exactly like that,
it was close. (YOU try writing in verse about loving
  your fat).

The point is, self-hate starts from outside,
and bigotry of all kinds is spread far and wide.
And until they come up with a self-hate vaccine,
let's help each other challenge the meme.

Self-love is a happier place to be dwelling;
let's make the choice now not to buy what they're selling.
A kiss of acceptance plus a loveable hug
can help beyond measure to battle this bug.
And while there's much I don't know, of this I am sure:
Body love and NOT hate is part of the cure.

PART X

LOVE

We were told when we were young that love was for slim people, that no one could possibly like us if we stayed fat. What we now derive from this perhaps well-intentioned advice was that the people who gave it didn't know what love was and didn't know how lovable fat people can be.

There are many kinds of love, and there are many kinds of people who love. As we write love poems, we create and recreate love in a larger, more inclusive realm and version. Love swells and flows and sings in us as we write.

Kathy, Frannie, Eileen, Durette

Kathy Barron

LOVE TALK*

I am in full bloom;
there is plenty of room for
everything you want.

*Espero que me
entiendes cuando te
digo te amo.*

I can be so bad.
I can be so very good.
Which do you prefer? ;)

Dare I speak the truth
of what lies within my heart?
Or will it scare you?

We seem to hear words
but rarely do we listen
to what's being said.

I appreciate
the wonderful gift of you
brightening my life.

I could play all day;
there is so much more to say
in a succinct way.

Just imagine what
people feel inside their hearts
if you withhold love.

I don't wear a bra.
It is not against the law.
Don't care if they droop.

Snowflakes at the door
pushed by raging winds at storm.
Won't you keep me warm?

Waves lapping at shore,
kissing and wetting the sand.
"I'll love you evermore."

Love is the answer.
Open your heart and share it.
Make a better world.

"Don't say what you think"
is the worst advice ever.
The truth sets you free.

I am not perfect.
Please do not judge me for it.
We all do our best.

Tell me how you feel;
my heart feels so tender now.
Please help me to heal.

It's been a long time
since I've considered in depth
my buried feelings.

Please don't be afraid;
I'm really not losing it.
I'm just exploring.

People feel so much
that they hide from everyone,
afraid to be judged.

Would you run away
if I told you how I feel?
Or would you hold me?

Sometimes we give up,
not knowing that we are close
to our heart's desire.

Bending to the sun,
plants eager for warmth and light,
like me loving you.

Puffy clouds floating
just above me in the sky.
I wish it was you.

Lavender flowers'
healing scent fills the air and
I am now reborn.

Animals do not
go hungry when there is food.
Why do we humans?

Raging river speak
to me, calm my stormy heart.
Wash away my tears.

The warmth of your breath
caresses my hungry skin;
I'm in love again.

Dust blowing across
an unpaved, forgotten road
like you touching me.

Life bursting forth and
death taming life. Wonder what
will tame my desire?

Kathy Barron

LOVE PLAY*

You can't love me
with one foot on the gas pedal, honey.
I need you to get out of the car.
I need you to stand with both feet on the ground,
using your leverage to push deeply into me;
you need to stay a while,
commit to connecting,
open up your heart and body
and immerse yourself in me.

Take the keys out of the ignition, baby;
this is going to take a while.
Leave your clothes in the car;
you won't need them.
Come swim in the pool of my love, sugar.
Let go of your worries and dive into me,
sink into me,
rest a moment in the sweet softness of my love.

Tell me what you need, darlin'.
How can I help you to relax,
let go of the past and future,
just be here now in my arms,
floating on the softness of my body,
letting yourself feel everything—
loved, wanted, vibrantly alive,
safe to express all of yourself
in the vast sea of my love.

Hold onto me tight, honey.
Let me feel your warm body
flush against mine,
your heart beating against my
gentle breasts,
your hardness pressing into my
pillow-soft belly,
your strong arms encircling me,
holding me in your sensual embrace.

That's it, baby.
And when your passion is spent,
just let yourself melt into
this cozy nest of warm bodies
that we have created,
knowing that you can always
find this place again with me.
There's no need to go rushing off,
no need to go searching;
you'll find everything you need
right here, lover.

Frannie Zellman

LOVE POEM

I prayed
that my fat muse
would steal you,
haul you roughly,
fill you with oaths
spoken without voice
in prayer
mouthed without breath

as she gave birth to angry poems
that you had

never spoken
but had cursed
beyond a last hope
out of sleeping.

Eileen Rosensteel

Size Matters

How big are you?
Cause honey, I like 'em big.
And I am not talking about
your egotistical,
in-your-dreams,
she-won't-be-able-to-tell,
internet-come-on
size.
I need to know that you are big enough for me.
I am a woman with
huge assets.
My skills are legendary.
And I am not wasting them on
small people
anymore.
Screw that!
If you are going to dance with me,
you had better be BIG.
So how big are you?

Kathy Barron

LOVE TALK II

Don't give me that soft love
that hinges on approval of how I look
or on how I live my life
or on what I do for you
or on expectations of who you think
I "should" be—or "could" be—
and falls into disappointment and judgment
if I turn out to be different from your image of me.

Don't give me that illusion of love
that scatters with the merest breeze,
dissipating into the nothingness
of which it is constructed
of social contrivances and conveniences,
all show and no substance,
leaving me alone, lost and cold,
when I most need you.

Give me that fierce love
that endures all things
and remains steady and strong
through all of the ups and downs, trials and tribulations,
and triumphs and mistakes of life,
that holds me with exquisitely tender hands
supporting me, cheering me, comforting me, steadily
loving me
whether I fly or fall—love me where I am.

Give me that solid love

that I can lean into and rest in,
that I can swing around and wrestle with
knowing it is flexible and unbreakable,
knowing it won't run away
and won't let me down
and won't let me drop into insignificance
and will be there—ready to hold me when I need it.

Don't give me that leeching love
that looks for the ways in which
I could benefit you
or reflect well upon you,
a scoresheet constantly tabulating
whether or not I am "worth it,"
the essence of me dismissed
as nothing more than a commodity.

Don't give me that ownership love
that looks at my body
and imagines where I could "improve,"
or that looks at my life
and fantasizes where I could be
more "impressive" or "successful,"
or that entertains the thought that you could
make better choices for my life than I do. Oh no, no!

Give me that free, unconditional love
that sees me just as I am
without filters of expectations and demands,
that welcomes and accepts me just as I am,
respecting my individuality and autonomy,
holding space for my growth and explorations,
encouraging my changes and my risks

and standing firmly with me through it all.

Give me that fierce, loyal, unending love,
that passionate, patient, unbreakable love,
that trusting, trustworthy, open, supportive love,
that powerful, committed, unyielding love,
that authentic, deep, wholehearted love.
Love me for real—or love me not at all.
I need love that I can depend on.
Give me love to hold on to.

Love Buzz*

The woman has voluptuous curves.
Her hair flows, glowing over her beautiful bosom.
Her cheeks are healthy, desirable.
Her nose and eyes the real disguise.

Her belly loves to be fat and delicious.
Her hips are enchanting, her vagina dancing.
She smiles at her full thighs and calves
and thinks of the fun she has had.

Her knees, they are the "bee's."
The buzz is all around.
Her feet are firmly on the ground.
Her lovely fat body is craved by her man.
He loves all of her again
and again.

Kathy Barron

LOVE TALK III*

Wake me with your kiss.
Trail your tongue along my skin.
Mouth explore my curves.

PART XI

FORGIVING

Finding the strength to forgive the people who literally belittled us is not easy, but it is necessary. Finding the words to forgive ourselves for thinking that we weren't worthy—of love, of life, of dreams—is even more difficult, and perhaps even more necessary.

Frannie, Lesleigh, Anne

Frannie Zellman

FORGIVENESS*

The door wanted no part of it.
It was a safe wooden door, or so it appeared.
In its infancy it had occupied
some shade that wood likes, on a continuum
between chestnut and pine.
In a crime against wooden doors everywhere,
it had been painted a cutesy, cheesy white
when it became a dorm bathroom door.
Its mute protest was expressed
in oh-so-quaint old-house-type
squeaks when some unthinking high or drunken student
attempted to open it quietly
or close it without falling down flat.

One late autumn morning a female student who resided
in the same house as the door
decided to shower.
Not asking permission of the door
but not dishonoring it,
she shut the door, not thinking that she was committing
any shocking act or crime by so doing.
She did all the showery things
one normally does with soap and water
and was preparing to open the shower curtain
and so begin the drying process
when faintly through the last streams
of falling drops, she thought she heard, of all things,
a knock.

Believing at first that her ears must have played
a trick on the rest of her—for who would be
so patently untoward
as to knock on the door when she—or anyone—
was involved in the showering process?—
she ignored what she felt must have been
some half-sound that pretended to be a knock
—a knock wannabe, as it were—
and completed the last
of her shower-related ablutions.
She was reaching for the towel,
as she was wont to do in such circumstances,
when it came again, the thud that communicated itself
as a knock to the person on the other side of the door.

If she could have, she would have engaged the door
and questioned it as to how it could have let
such an unexpected and possibly unwelcome
sliver of sound through its solidly although woebegonely
    white
wooden premises
during a time when quiet, if not silence, should have
    rendered
the bathroom space sacrosanct.
But she was not aware of any capacity on the part of the
    door
for speech or personal or sociocultural analysis
pertaining to the use of the bathroom area
by more than one person at a given time.
So she simply said, in response to what
she had now identified beyond a shadow
of a doubt as a knock, "I'm almost finished
in here."

FORGIVING   *121*

There was an instance in which silence reigned
in the throb of a heartbeat,
taking over the door and the bathroom
and the house and even the autumn wind
that whistled and worried the cracks
that had appeared throughout the years,
claimed by the venerable house that occupied stony
ground
amid stories and legends
that grew up around it according to students
who occupied it for a short space in the lives
of humans, then gave way to other students
who no doubt embellished the tales
the way the people who built the house
had once embellished it with the latest
coverlets and lavish overdoor *vêtements*
as well as mantelpiece fixings and fenestrations.

Then a voice invaded from the other side of the door:
"It's me."
"It"—personal pronoun used here as an identifier. "Me"—
personal pronoun used
here as object.
Not having been schooled in the use of English as a
spoken medium,
the door had nothing to say on the subject
and stayed mute.

The problem is that the young woman
on the other side of the door
had been thoroughly schooled in speaking,
but the two words, uttered by someone familiar to her,

threw her into confusion and made part of her dizzy.
Looking askance at the door, she said, "Hi."

"Look," the voice continued,
"I have to pee. The other bathroom upstairs
is occupied."
"I'll be out of here in a minute," she repeated.
"But I need to use it now," the voice insisted.

"Um—" was what emerged from her throat
after half a second.
"Come on," the voice said. "Just let me in
and go right back into the shower."
"Well," is what her mouth managed
to produce after another half a second.
"Are you afraid that I will be led
by the sight of that lush body of yours
to commit indiscretions?" the voice purred.

Now this is what she would have wished
to explain to the door, if not to the questioner:
"I have wanted the person who goes with this voice
for two years. I can imagine his hands
soaping all of me starting with my neck
and shoulders and generous breasts and going lower
to my happy place and my soft and wishful thighs.
But I cannot ask him in this particular
circumstance because it is just possible
that he has in mind simply to relieve himself.
The bigger fool I if he refused such an overture
and left me embarrassed and unable
to communicate easily with him
and others

who would puzzle out what went awry between us."

The door, to its credit, said nothing
in the rush of silence that floated
between her and the person
on the other side of it.
She would never tell a soul
of the flash of exquisite agony
that enveloped her entire body and mind
and being
and which her spirit self would carry
for the rest of its lifetimes.

"Okay," is what issued finally from her mouth.

She turned the doorknob and quickly
made her way back into the moist
and warm enclosure of the shower.
Safe, too safe behind the curtain,
she turned on the water
so that she would not know.

She washed and soaped and washed again,
rigidly working the soap up and down
all of the softness she was and owned
and still not knowing
in her ultimate confusion
if she wanted the curtain, blameless
bland plastic presence,
to be thrown aside,
and not knowing in her self-doubt
if he wanted her,
a tall top-heavy woman, no bones prominent

anywhere, flesh padding the parts of her
that curved
in and out and around
and wanted to be played with
but could never state such
to the voice which had requested
their quiescence.

She pushed and soaped and soaped
some more, making some of the places
red with her insistence.

At last, when she felt that she could no longer
keep skin on her body if she were to rub it more,
she shut off the water.

She listened. In the heartbeat that followed
lived only silence.

She yanked aside the shower curtain.

The tile and the rest of the room
bore no signs of recent use.
No invisible strains of warmth
or the being that held them
or the voice that spun them.

The door, white and mute
as before, was not about
to receive her heart or its wishing.
It was, after all, a door,
and even with the changes
it had endured,

was not about to take up
human moral dilemmas
or unreasonable importuning.
It stood, not giving any signs
of embarrassment or ambivalence
or deceit.

Still confused, her wishes still invading
all those soft, secret places
that wishes know all too well how to capture,
she dried herself slowly, giving her breasts
and her happy place
and her unflat stomach a few extra pats,
as if they were pets who needed to be indulged.
As the day went by, the vague unsettlement
of yearning left,
and she resumed her blithely unwary student ways,
doing what students do when they can no longer
avoid the library.

Through all this the door held to its wooden
unyielding aura and brooked no difference
in attitude or bearing.
It continued to serve faithfully
in its post as dorm bathroom door
until the house was torn down
ten years after.

If you walk by now,
you see a new admin building
where the old house stood,
nary a sign or hint of wanting.
The door went to door heaven

long ago, part of a lawn
near new dorms.

Such is the cycle.
The woman and the voice attached
to the man who confused her
have not spoken for years.
An occasional remembrance,
a shorter regret, and then it all goes again.

Autumn, if it knows what minds do not,
speaks only with the wind.

Within her soft thick body
a vague shrug,
as if that's the only thing
that could point at, then settle
the matter.

You might call it forgiveness.

Lesleigh Owen

SOFT

How compelling can a poem without angst be?
I told myself not to lift my fingers from this keyboard,
but even fevers need fed
and eyes require cleaning.
I don't operate on batteries anymore,
although when I sleep, I have been known to
make a suspicious buzzing noise.

The press and release of routine;
I crave the resentment and comfort of it all.
Without ritual, how could I free myself
to think thoughts that remain unvoiced
and realizations that I forget within the hour?

How can anyone love grays and browns
when blacks and whites shine and stab and pierce
like teeth through flesh?
Is there a strength in being common,
being pretty,
being accommodating,
being the third smartest person
in the world?
Or maybe it's the be-ing
that pumps potency into the world
in quiet gasps and blinks.

I used to scatter violence in my poems,
up above the page so high,
shards twinkling, twinkling

in the sky.
I don't miss
or covet that walnut-colored, blocky pain,
checking my hair for genetic hints,
white and springy impulses in an otherwise
soft tangle of
innocuous brown curls.
The illusion of power in abuse,
of control in pain,
of devotion in jealousy:
My strength rumbles up from the ground,
rotund and rich
with triple chins and enough cellulite in the belly
to pad the heads of ten or more cats
and the not-as-innocuous brown curls
of my Prince Charming.
I find inspiration in silence
and songs in sighs.

Did you know?
The strongest substances are also the softest.

And because I can't tell you any other way,
he hurt me for ten years.
And no, it's not okay when you interrupt me—
even when I say it is.
And I am not broken.
And all those poems I wrote about raw lips gaping,
screaming and singing and rhyming
into vast, dusty silences?
Learn to take a hint.
And I largely dated men because
I wanted my mom to be proud of me.

And most days I cherish this body—
think it should be memorialized in latex
in some museum
for the masses to rub against and dream—
but some days I'd like to revel and roll,
with a jellied messiness that would horrify the nuns,
inside a thin privilege I will never know.
And guess what, Mom:
Prince Charming was never a boy.

Anne S. Kaplan

HOPE FOR THE HATERS

Hey, you! Yeah, you—
    the one who hates me
    calls me ugly names
    doesn't know me yet
    wishes me dead/gone/invisible
        just because I'm fat.

Who did that to you?
    Who stole your soul,
        slashed your heart?
    Who never taught you
        divinity in every being?
    Who never showed you
        how to love yourself?

I can choose to ignore you.
    Knowing the ugliness
    is yours, not mine, I can
    walk, dance or swim away,
        allow you no impact on my life,
        and have none on yours.

Or, I could choose
    to return your hate,
    expect you to know better,
    fume that you do not.
    My rage at you could
        fuel my voice.

Instead, I pity you.
    I see your tin-man hole

feel your hollow ego
ache your poor parenting.

And I know your loathing to be
your mirror's reflection,
as you feel no respect,
compassion, or love,
for yourself.

Some say I ought not bother,
wasting breath and energy on you.
Perhaps I am naive, an idealist, when
I try to kindle a light in the dark,
as Martin urged us so long ago.

Instead of blaming you,
knowing you were raised
malnourished
on a diet of hate,
I fan within my own soul
a flicker of hope.
Maybe, you really do not know?

I hope that you will see the light
of love, compassion,
thus come to know your own
specialness, your beauty.
Celebrate your divinity.
See the divine in all.

In finding compassion for you,
I hope you find your own heart.
Will you languish in hatred,
or find light, peace, love?

Part XII

GODDESS

We celebrate the goddess, the eternal woman, in us daily and nightly, finding her in our dreams, hopes and visions. We celebrate our wonderful fat goddess. You can see her in clay figurines recovered from ancient caves. We celebrate her power not over us, but in us.

Mary, Eileen, Anne, Lesleigh, Frannie

Mary Ray Worley

ANCIENT DREAMS

Ancient dreams
awake in the longing
of the night.
Who am I
when I close
my eyes?
I am the
revered body,
the sanctified
form.
I am the
aspiration
of tribes.
I am pride
overflowing
into bright days
of abundance.
I am the
awakening of
ancient dreams.

Eileen Rosensteel

FLESH EVERLASTING

My flesh was,
before,
before becoming my body.
This flesh made
other beings
alive.
Flesh becoming flesh.
Body decaying,
transforming
into
again.

Anne S. Kaplan

THE GODDESS (SELF-PORTRAIT)

The Goddess stands at the edge,
    suspended
between earth and water,
    day and night,
    reserve and ebullience,
    wind and stillness,
    shadow and light.

Arms spread wide,
    she opens doors to love,
    invites us to join her
    in celebrating the divine:
    rounded fullness of our
    beautiful bodies.

Lesleigh Owen

MAKING WAVES

Lips like ocean waves,
tummy whose swells and ripples
I ride to the sea.

Frannie Zellman

RADIANCE
To My Mother

Plump and radiant,
you adored them all
with your eyes.
Flowers in your hair,
you twirled your fan
from admirer to admirer
and led the boys
a merry dance
as you jumped from one
to the other
and winked at some
you didn't care to know.

One summer morning
you raised your arms
and yawned
into being
another crop of young men
to appraise,
to render helpless
in your presence,
turning, Circe-like,
humans
into sea swine
who lost their speech
and instead
could only make raw, rasping sounds
of love.

Tiny, thin now,
you stay beautiful
not just in memory
but in the eyes of those
who meet your eyes
and report back
to their officers
that yes, the danger
still exists.
And by god and goddess,
what a woman to win
and to keep
if you can avoid the spell.

But of course
the fun lies still
in bringing down
the danger of your spell,
and in the allure
of singing their aches
to you
without words
in a far, unknown place.

And for a few,
if they were once easy with words,
in trying to find the right sounds
to capture the essence
of your eyes
all at once,
without fading.

PART XIII

ACCEPTANCE

Finally, after our journeys through minds and hearts, we come to the hard-won, always fragile relief of acceptance—not from others, but from ourselves. All the anger, the jeers—the personal demons of which we let go along the way—find us greeting the space in which we find peace and sometimes contentment within our lives, our bodies, ourselves, and with people in our lives.

We have lived and learned, suffered, loved, sighed, rebelled and understood some of the patterns of our lives. Sometimes we related directly as fat people to what occurred at different parts of our lives, and sometimes we thought of ourselves simply as people going through our days and accomplishing the personal and public tasks necessary to order and complete them.

And now, not all the time, but surprisingly more often than not, we bask in the determined, not-so-quiet glow of our acceptance of our fat, good bodies and selves.

Eileen, Anne, Kathy, Lesleigh

Eileen Rosensteel

ALICE

She quite simply was
never the right size.
Too big, too small.
The silly girl
had been them all.
It was far too hard
to figure out
when she really didn't know
who she was.
For once you know who,
size is no longer an issue.
Since you are far too busy being you.

Anne Kaplan

PEACE

Dark room, open curtains,
bathing in light of full moon.
Without judgment or comment,
in our glorious roundness,
she and I simply, peacefully, be.

Kathy Barron

No Competition

There is no competition,
you know,
between my body
and yours—
or hers—
or his.

There is no measuring stick
against which
we must stand
to determine
beauty, lovability, desirability
or worthiness.

There is no comparison
that has
any significance,
nothing true or real
which separates us.
Hierarchies are false.

There is only this:
the warm, living,
breathing, pulsing
life force that
moves within the miracles
that we call "bodies."

Anne S. Kaplan

MASSAGE

Strong, gentle hands knead
my rolls over meat and bones.
Body sighs in pleasure.

Lesleigh Owen

RAINBOW

Gentle and wise, my
belly arcs like a rainbow,
blotting out the sky.

Anne S. Kaplan

WHALE

I swim for the joy.
"Look at the fat whale!" you yell.
"Thank you!" I reply.

BIOGRAPHIES

KATHY BARRON

I feel so different about my body and my life now than I ever did before. It is challenging to put into words, but I'll do my best.

My roundness and rolls used to be a source of shame for me. Now, when my lover grips them as he plunges into me, I have come to see them as sensual, beautiful, desirable, delicious, and very wanted. My body doesn't feel like my enemy anymore, keeping me from the love and sex that I have craved my whole life—instead, it is my dear friend, enabling me to experience and delight in so much pleasure and intimacy and wonderful connection.

I used to think that if I could get thin enough, then I would be desirable. But I really understand now that everyone has different tastes—and while there are many people to whom I hold no appeal at all, there are also many people who would be delighted to be intimate with me.

I'm only interested in people who love and adore me exactly as I am. Why would anybody settle for less than that?

Oh, how I delight in my body. My chubby, chunky, rolly, warm, tender, sensual fat body.

The joy I have in my body at this time in my life— the pleasure that I accept for my body, the delicious lovers that I welcome into my body—I could not have even imagined this for myself at one time in my life. It didn't come all at once—and it hasn't been all easy. And I'm not completely immune to society's body-hating messages. But most of the time in my life, I am in love with my Self and with my beautiful, miraculous body. And I am so grateful to be exactly who and how I am.

Imagine, if you will, being at a beautiful resort with the sun shining on the sparkling blue water of the pool while a small waterfall flows and people of all sizes, shapes and colors lounge, swim and walk around naked. There is chatter and laughter and music. There is no self-consciousness or body supremacy. People simply enjoy the sun and each other.

Hop naked onto a bike, ride past a beautiful lake, down streets lined with trees and beautiful plants—and naked people everywhere, gardening, playing tennis, golfing, living their lives. That's where I live. And I am so enormously grateful for that!

I wish that I could adequately articulate the difference that becoming a nudist has made in my body image and my self-concept. And, for people who aren't familiar with nudism, let me just say that nudism and sexuality are not the same thing. There are strict rules at American Association of Nude Recreation (AANR) affiliated nudist resorts and facilities in order to keep them family friendly and non-sexual.

Nudism is about enjoying your natural body and feeling free and comfortable in your own skin. And since so many people are ashamed of their bodies in some way, I think that nudism is one of the most healing things people can embrace for their body image and self-acceptance.

My changing body image has been a fundamental part of my growth. It has allowed a level of self-acceptance that has created a freedom in my life based in worthiness and self love.

I can barely even remember what it was like to have my life run by how much I could eat—or paying attention to trying to control the size of my body—rather than just enjoying and loving my body as it is and eating whatever appeals to me based on hunger and my own satisfaction. I don't think about how much or how little to eat—I just eat what feels good in my body.

It's so strange for me that other people are still stuck in the old paradigm of trying to control their weight/size—and watching them struggle through all of the fluctuations and misery. I would like to help people overcome that; that kind of suffering is so unnecessary and unhealthy.

Of course, feeling good in your body and releasing any feelings of shame and/or unworthiness will have a positive effect on your sexuality, too—at least, if that is desired. For me, that is something that has been highly desired and is now welcomed into my life.

After several decades of feeling that nobody would want to look at me or be interested in me sexually, my changing self-image has allowed me to see how wrong I was. And that my body is a gift. And that I am a desirable woman, capable of attracting wonderful lovers and experiencing depths of intimacy and sexuality that I had only dreamed of until my late 40s.

As I approach my 50th birthday, I am finding the world of sexuality opening up for me in ways that I hadn't allowed myself to experience before because I had bought into this society's messages that I wasn't "good enough"—that I wasn't pretty enough, that I had the wrong body type—all of the lies that are heaped upon us to make us believe that we are unworthy of love and affection and great, hot sex so that we are preoccupied with our "flaws" and can be sold "cures" of weight loss and makeup and fashion, all of the things that will supposedly make us finally worthy. Fact: We are already worthy and we don't have to change a thing!

My new course in life is to work with women on freeing their bodies, minds, and emotions—to help them reclaim their bodies, and their personal and sexual power. My career is practicing Myofascial Release for the physical part of it, getting the body unstuck—which impacts the mind and emotions as well—and I am also working on writing sex-positive, body-positive novels and books, and doing some coaching with some of my clients around body image and freedom.

Lots of exciting plans as I move toward my sixth decade of life!

ANNE S. KAPLAN, PH.D., CPCC

Known around the Internet as "coach anne," I am a life coach and healing consultant. Having previously worn many other "hats" (including neuroscientist and computer programmer), I am now living my life purpose by empowering others. And am doing so, finally, as an openly fat and proud woman.

Via AmpleAliveness™ I serve owners of microbusinesses and women ready to reclaim their power from the word "fat." My blog and website at http://amplealiveness.com are an evolving invitation to join me on the journey from self-loathing to self-respect, -appreciation, and -celebration; from despair to hope; from life deferred to some mythical day to life lived full-out in the present.

In addition to size acceptance/body diversity and Health at Every Size® (HAES), some of my other interests include healing approaches such as ZPoint and EFT, spirituality, travel (especially via cruise ship), size- and mobility accessibility, community-building, public speaking, wellness, self-care, body wisdom, Sudoku, ethical science and compassionate medicine, and heart-based living. My husband of 35+ years and I, currently empty-nesters and owned by two beagles, are hoping to one day become grandparents.

People who know me now find me to be enormously caring, passionate, funny, serious, short, fat, earthy, intuitive, spiritual, an ADDult, and, every once in a while, wise; and I defy anyone—including myself—to say that "fat" is the most important word in that list. But it used to be, and I used to be a very different person.

For much of my life, "fat" was the only way I thought of myself, along with all I was taught "fat" meant—ugly, unlovable, unworthy—if you're reading this, you know what I mean. I was lonely and sad and angry and lost.

My shift towards a more accepting sense of self began with books like *Fat is a Feminist Issue, Overcoming Overeating,* and Geneen Roth's series. However, I arrived at my most significant turning point (described in a poem by that name in the first volume of *Fat Poets Speak*) not that long ago, and only after hitting bottom.

The poem starts off very sad (as did I), but the sadness is not the point—rather, it's how despair, and survival, and the rage that was born from it, and the divine undercurrent to all of that, helped make me who I am today. Without having touched that darkness, I'd not have had that quantum shift and spiritual awakening.

One of the things born in the aftermath was my ferocious dedication to my own self- and size acceptance, and the calling to serve people (instead of statistics and bits & bytes) and, eventually, people of size. The slogan mentioned in the poem—given to me that week in a dream—is the same one I often use to sign my emails:

"Become all you are, today; don't wait to be less."

LESLEIGH OWEN

In the third grade, I penned A Great American Novel. Maybe not "The," but definitely "A."

See, Shelly had an unhappy life. Then she found a time machine and accidentally stranded herself in the past. I mean, like, the past-past with dinosaurs and stuff. Luckily some guy named Brian had stumbled across the same time machine and got stranded there, too. They looked and looked—with the help of their new pet, Dyno—to find a way home. Finally they realized there was just no going back. They gave up searching, got married, and had lots of babies. Dyno did, too.

Oh, and there were lots of hand-drawn pictures, most featuring Shelly with increasingly longer hair and with ever-more littl'uns, all clad in saber-toothed-tiger skins. (What does an eight-year-old know about historical anachronisms?)

Thus began my literary career.

By the age of thirteen I was penning 200-page paranormal romance novels and, much to everyone's dismay, some really angsty sonnets. My schoolmates knew me as Lesleigh the Writer. My family knew me as the introvert who spent all her spare time with pencil and notebook in hand.

A very few years after the angsty-sonnet phase wore itself out (you're welcome), I jumped into queer activism, which led naturally to feminist activism and eventually into movements around fat pride and body diversity. Now I find myself pretty passionate about most political topics, although those first three remain very close to my heart. Luckily my job as a sociology instructor allows me to talk to students about how and why to blend elements of social justice with social theory—and they pay me for it!

I have the best job in the world, but I'm the first to admit I had to work my ample bee-hind off (not literally, thank goodness!) to get there. During my college years and the endless studying and writing, I couldn't bring myself to pen more than a poem or two a year, let alone write novels. I channeled my love of writing into jotting an award-winning feminist opinion column. Then there came master's papers and the dissertation, which I ashamedly admit I didn't actually hate; however, I had no time for Shelly, Dyno, and their kind. Sadly, I put Lesleigh the Writer on ice until—well, until that fateful NAAFA workshop I attended in 2006. The workshop that helped birth the Fat Poets' Society and, eventually, the first *Fat Poets Speak*.

Lesleigh the Writer is back, baby! She was reborn in 2006 with a renewed love of poetry and fiction and a heapin' helpin' of learnin' tucked under her belt. Since then, and under the gentle and loving guidance of Frannie Zellman, my friend and mentor, the poems have flowed from my fingers.

Three years ago, at the none-too-gentle urging of my older sister, author Lauri J Owen, I decided to try my hand once again at writing novels. I wrote a novelette that became *Hunted*, the basis for my Hunted Series. *Hunted Past* and *Hunted Dreams* have followed, and I'm working on a fourth book right now, as well as a short story entitled

"A Hunted Holiday." I publish my paranormal romance under the pseudonym Elle Hill, mostly because it creeps me out to think of my students Googling me, finding my books, and discovering their sociology instructor actually knows what sex is. Ewww!

As I say all over my promotional author stuff, I am a not-so-mild-mannered college instructor by day and a writer by night. Living in South Dakota with my sister and our cats and near my cherished partner, I lead a happy and healthy life. And while Shelly remains unpublished, she was the first of many strong sheroes whose stories have taken shape under the movements of my fingers over keys. Sometimes, especially when writing poetry, that shero is me.

I would like to offer my most loving thanks to Peggy Elam to giving the Fat Poets' Society a space—and sugar, we take up a whole lot of it!—to share our songs. My thanks also to the loving and talented women and men of the Fat Poets' Society who have read and critiqued all of the poetry we include in this volume. Special thanks to my beloved Kathy Barron, Corinna Makris, Anne Kaplan, and Mary Worley, the original and core group of the FPS. And most especially I offer thanks to Frannie Zellman, whose passion, leadership, and sheer literary talent continue to inspire us all.

And thank you, lovely reader, for buying this book and helping us celebrate the beautiful possibilities of fat bodies.

If you're interested in hearing more of my thoughts, I invite you to my author blog:

http://ellehillauthor.blogspot.com/

Eileen Rosensteel

Eileen Rosensteel is a bodacious Bohemian committed to embodying Goddess. Finding inspiration in stories of forgotten foremothers, sacred moments, and community, she creates poetry, performance art and healing rituals.

Her portfolio includes a show about the fat ladies of the circus, dancing in a non-normative body, and poetry about what it's like being a fat woman in today's society.

She stirs life up from her hometown of Madison, Wisconsin. Her work has been shared on stage as well as in *We'Moon, Breadcrumb Scabs,* and *Madison Magazine.*
Connect with her on Facebook or at
www.fatladyshow.com.

Mary Ray Worley

Mary Ray Worley is a freelance copy editor who works on books for university presses. She leads the music for and coordinates her church's service in Spanish and lives in Madison, Wisconsin with her husband, Tom, and Smudgie the cat. Her blog, *The Worley Dervish,* focuses primarily on Wisconsin politics with frequent forays into feminism and women's rights.

Mary plays guitar and sings with the daily Solidarity Sing Along at the Wisconsin state capitol every opportunity she gets, and writes songs for the sing along as well. She also participates in a weekly group-singing adventure known as the Madison Song Circle, and is overjoyed to be part of a community that loves to sing.

FRANNIE ZELLMAN

Philosophy is
fat people finally in
their own skin poems.

Not deep. Just shouting.
Banshees strong and round. Dancing
moon and whirling sun.

What I am. A cat
in one life. Fluffy trouble.
Fish heads and cream licks.

So far to have come.
Body shame, body hate snaps.
Taste me quick, you fools.

One day worlds will know.
Now we fight. Our words, our swords.
Our offering, hope.

I wrote *FatLand: A Novel.* Peggy Elam, Ph.D. at Pearlsong Press—our redoubtable publisher—was intelligent and far-seeing enough to publish it in 2009. A second volume, *FatLand: The Early Days,* has recently been published, also by Pearlsong Press. Both envision life in a society that forbids scales, talk of diets, and weight-based discrimination. Peggy was also deeply supportive of the first volume of *Fat Poets Speak: Voices of the Fat Poets' Society,* which Pearlsong Press published in 2009. This second volume, *Fat Poets Speak 2: Living and Loving Fatly,* also comes to you from

Pearlsong Press.

I have created a blog for The FatLand Trilogy and will also create one for the Fat Poets Speak Series, of which I am the editor as well as a contributor. Thus we will be able to talk about "fat" fiction, a genre which has grown wonderfully in the last ten years, and "fat" poetry, which is starting to attract more and more fans intrigued by the idea of poets being proud enough in their own skins to write about what it is like to go through days and lives in the USA as fat people.

Thank you for reading what we have written and possibly thinking about it and finding yourself in some private, yet comforting alley stoop where we have been and where you now join us. Sit with us a while and see who we are and how you intersect with us.

http://FrannieZellman.blogspot.com
http://fatpoetsspeak.blogspot.com

NEW VOICES

DURETTE HAUSER

Durette Hauser is a tax accountant who lives in Laingsburg, Michigan. She has a loving husband, Russell, whom she has been with for 25 years. She has owned her own accounting and tax business since 1989.
She loves traveling, trying new foods and recipes, reading, swimming, yoga, bluegrass music, living life to the fullest, her body, and attending loving retreats.

Her first positive exposure to fat acceptance was reading the book *Wake Up, I'm Fat!* by Camryn Manheim. She first attended an Abundia retreat in 2004. She had never heard of Health at Every Size (HAES) until that retreat. The very idea that being fat was acceptable totally rocked her world. Since then she has taken a journey on the Spiral of Acceptance towards better health and happiness. She hopes to see more women learn about the concept of Health at Every Size.

The annual Abundia Retreat (www.abundia.org) is the perfect place to come and be loved by many other fat women and to learn to love yourself more.

DEB LEMIRE

Deb Lemire is founder and artistic director of Queen Bee Productions, a professional organization producing creative works that advocate for women. QBP offers workshops, talks and performance presentations that focus on issues important to women, including body and size acceptance.

Her original piece "For Beauty's Sake" was commissioned by the Multi-Service Eating Disorders Association (MEDA) for their 10th anniversary. Deb also presented at the Endangered Species: Women Summit in New York in March 2011. She has been honored for her achievements by the National Organization for Women, YWCA, and the Akron Women's History Project. She is an advocate for the Health At Every Size approach on her Ohio school district's wellness policy committee.

Deb was instrumental in the development of the bylaws of the Association for Size Diversity and Health (ASDAH), is the immediate Past President of ASDAH, and currently chairs the organization's public policy committee.

DR. DEAH SCHWARTZ

Dr. Deah Schwartz has more than 20 years' experience using therapeutic arts, music, drama and recreation activities in a variety of clinical and educational settings with clients ranging in age from five to 80+. She has a doctorate in education, a B.A. in theater, an M.S .in therapeutic recreation, and an M.A. in creative arts education, and is a nationally certified recreation therapist. In addition, Dr. Schwartz studied art therapy at the College of Notre Dame in Belmont, California for two years and taught expressive arts and recreation therapy at San Francisco State University for ten years.

This background, coupled with her fervent belief in size acceptance, has resulted in her co-authoring the *Leftovers* workbook/DVD set, a unique expressive arts therapy curriculum for therapists and educators training therapists in the fields of eating disorders and body dissatisfaction. Deah also has a blog, called *Tasty Morsels,* that promotes size acceptance and Health at Every Size, and recently published *Dr. Deah's Calmanac: Your Interactive Monthly Guide for Cultivating a Positive Body Image.*

Read more at
http://www.arttherapyblog.com/about/about-dr-deah-schwartz/#ixzz2bAVACore

M. M. Stein

Mary M. Stein (that's me) is a fat and sassy Midwestern gal. I was born and raised in Northeast Ohio, earning my B.A. and M.A. in English from the University of Akron. I have 20 years' experience in the corporate sector working for local companies and Fortune 500s in customer service, public relations, sales, advertising, and broadcast media. Currently I teach English composition at the University of Akron and Stark State College, in addition to writing poetry, fiction, nonfiction, and a weekly blog for More of Me to Love (www.moreofmetolove.com).

Among my many passions is living and teaching acceptance, especially size acceptance. I hope to inform as many everyday Americans as I can that the issue of size is not an issue at all, but merely a distraction from the real issues such as the decline in public education and accessibility to higher education, and our infrastructure, economy, and healthcare system.

About Pearlsong Press

Pearlsong Press is an independent publishing company dedicated to providing books and resources that entertain while expanding perspectives on the self and the world. The company was founded by psychologist Peggy Elam, Ph.D. in 2003.

You can purchase this and other Pearlsong books at www.pearlsong.com or your favorite bookstore. Keep up with us through our blog at www.pearlsongpress.com as we promote health, happiness and social justice at every size.

Nonfiction

Acceptable Prejudice? Fat, Rhetoric & Social Justice
& *Talking Fat: Health vs. Persuasion in the War on Our Bodies*
by Lonie McMichael, Ph.D.
Hiking the Pack Line: Moving from Grief to a Joyful Life
by Bonnie M. Shapbell
A Life Interrupted: Living with Brain Injury
by Louise Mathewson
ExtraOrdinary: An End of Life Story Without End
by Michele Tamaren & Michael Wittner
Love is the Thread: A Knitting Friendship by Leslie Moïse, Ph.D.
Fat Poets Speak: Voices of the Fat Poets' Society
edited by Frannie Zellman
Ten Steps to Loving Your Body (No Matter What Size You Are)
by Pat Ballard
Beyond Measure: A Memoir About Short Stature & Inner Growth
by Ellen Frankel
*Taking Up Space: How Eating Well & Exercising Regularly
Changed My Life* by Pattie Thomas, Ph.D. with
Carl Wilkerson, M.B.A. (foreword by Paul Campos)
*Off Kilter: A Woman's Journey to Peace with Scoliosis, Her Mother
& Her Polish Heritage* by Linda C. Wisniewski
Unconventional Means: The Dream Down Under
by Anne Richardson Williams

Splendid Seniors: Great Lives, Great Deeds by Jack Adler

Fiction

FatLand & *FatLand: The Early Days*—Volumes I & II of
The FatLand Trilogy by Frannie Zellman
Heretics: A Love Story & *The Singing of Swans*—novels
about the divine feminine by Mary Saracino
Judith—a novel by Leslie Moïse
The Season of Lost Children—a novel by Karen Blomain
Fatropolis—paranormal adventure by Tracey L. Thompson
*The Falstaff Vampire Files, Bride of the Living Dead, Larger Than
Death, Large Target, At Large* & *A Ton of Trouble*—paranormal
adventure, romantic comedy & Josephine Fuller mysteries
by Lynne Murray
Fallen Embers & *Blowing Embers*—Books 1 & 2 of
The Embers Series, paranormal romance by Lauri J Owen
The Program & *The Fat Lady Sings*—suspense & young adult
novels by Charlie Lovett
Syd Arthur—a novel by Ellen Frankel
Measure By Measure—a romantic romp with the fabulously fat
by Rebecca Fox & William Sherman

Romance Novels & Short Stories Featuring Big Beautiful Heroines

by Pat Ballard, the Queen of Rubenesque Romances:
ASAP Nanny: A Novella | *Dangerous Love* | *The Best Man*
Abigail's Revenge | *Dangerous Curves Ahead: Short Stories*
Wanted: One Groom | *Nobody's Perfect* | *His Brother's Child*
A Worthy Heir
by Rebecca Brock—*The Giving Season*
& by Judy Bagshaw—*Kiss Me, Nate!* & *At Long Last, Love*

Healing the World One Book at a Time